Susie Mountain is a Scottish Family ⌐ ᴧberdeen. She
has been accredited as a specialist in Faᵣ ⌐y the Law Society
of Scotland. An Associate at Brodies LLᵣ ᴧe acts for clients in a
huge variety of matters, including financial provision on divorce or
dissolution of civil partnerships, pre/post-nuptial agreements, child
law and of course advising on the rights of cohabitants. She is regularly instructed in high value cases and enjoys appearing in courts
across Scotland. Susie is passionate about educating younger lawyers
entering the profession. She tutors on the Diploma in Legal Practice,
is a young person mentor and speaks at seminars both in person and
online.

A Practical Guide to Cohabitation and the Law in Scotland

A Practical Guide to Cohabitation and the Law in Scotland

Susie Mountain
Solicitor
MA (Hons) LLB DLP

Law Brief Publishing

Published 2020 by Law Brief Publishing, an imprint of Law Brief Publishing Ltd
30 The Parks
Minehead
Somerset
TA24 8BT

www.lawbriefpublishing.com

Paperback: 978-1-912687-99-2

Huge and heartfelt thanks must go to all of the many family, friends and colleagues who have supported me with wisdom, patience and cups of tea during writing. I feel incredibly lucky to be surrounded by so many kind and talented people.

To the mini Mountains… apologies for all of the late bed times over the last few months.

Not forgetting Eric the dog for keeping my feet warm and taking me out for walks when I got stuck on tricky chapters!

Finally, many thanks to Tim and Garry at Law Brief Publishing for the opportunity and encouragement. I am extremely grateful.

CONTENTS

INTRODUCTION: AN APT TIME

The Office of National Statistics reports that there were approximately 273,000 cohabiting households in Scotland in 2019[1]. Cohabitation is on the rise and it is therefore an apt time for a) the Scottish Law Commission to consult on the reform of Scots cohabitation law and b) the publication of this book.

In Scotland we are ahead of our counterparts in the other UK jurisdictions, providing our cohabitants with a far greater degree of protection. That does not mean that more cannot be done – far from it – but where there may be the possibility of forum shopping Scotland should certainly be considered as the preferred jurisdiction (within the UK, at least) for the party seeking to bring a claim.

The Family Law (Scotland) Act 2006 (hereinafter referred to throughout this book as "the 2006 Act") brought in protection for cohabiting parties where previously little existed. Cohabitants were previously required to establish "marriage by cohabitation with habit and repute" (a remedy available only to those who were genuinely believed by third parties to be married), or were left to pursue claims, where possible, under the law of unjustified enrichment. Despite the fact that the 2006 Act has now been in force for a number of years, this is still an often head scratching area of Scots Law about which the general public appear to be relatively ill informed.

At the time of writing, we are in the midst of the global Covid-19 pandemic. Rarely a videoconference dinner party goes by without

---

1   https://www.ons.gov.uk/peoplepopulationandcommunity/ birthsdeathsandmarriages/families/bulletins/familiesandhouseholds/2019

talk of an impending tidal wave of divorce/dissolution cases as lockdown eases or, perhaps even more horrifyingly, a post-Covid baby boom. Further likely consequences include parties moving their beloved into their home at an accelerated pace to keep themselves aligned with ever shifting government guidelines; or parties who had intended to formalise their relationships putting those plans on hold for an indefinite period as venues close and social gatherings continue to be restricted. It seems inevitable that a further surge in the number of cohabiting households may result.

The law here is correct to the writer's knowledge as at 30th September 2020.

CHAPTER ONE
ABOLITION OF MARRIAGE
BY COHABITATION WITH
HABIT AND REPUTE

Scots Law on cohabitation was brought into the 21st Century with the enactment of the 2006 Act which came into force on 4 May 2006. The 2006 Act took great leaps forward in providing additional legal protection to those who may previously have been left with very little by way of remedy following the death of their cohabiting partner or the termination of their relationship. The sections predominantly applicable to cohabitation are found at ss. 25 to 29. However, this chapter will consider the abolition of "marriage by cohabitation with habit and repute" and the limited circumstances in which such a "marriage" may still be established.

The common law concept of "marriage by habit and repute" (or "irregular marriage") provides for parties to be treated as spouses (therefore falling within the scope of the legal provisions available to divorcing spouses under the Family Law Scotland Act 1985 and the applicable law on succession). Section 3 of the 2006 Act is entitled "abolition of marriage by cohabitation with habit and repute". However, this is somewhat misleading. Although subsection (1) states that *"the rule of law by which marriage may be constituted by cohabitation with habit and repute shall cease to have effect"[1],* this is expanded upon in subsections (2), (3) and (4) which provide for certain exceptions.

---

1   Family Law (Scotland) Act 2006 (2006, asp 2), section 3 (1)

Subsection 2: No Retrospective Effect

> *"3 (2) Nothing in subsection (1) shall affect the application of the rule in relation to cohabitation with habit and repute where the cohabitation with habit and repute –*
>
> (a) *ended before the commencement of this section ('commencement');*
>
> (b) *began before, but ended after, commencement; or*
>
> (c) *began before, and continues after, commencement.[2]"*

The law is not applied retrospectively. When practitioners are considering a cohabitation which commenced prior to 4 May 2006, it is of crucial importance that consideration is given as to whether it may be possible to establish a marriage by cohabitation with habit and repute, which may lead to a more favourable outcome for the client. The correct procedure in that event is to raise an action for declarator and to provide sufficient evidence to support the position. This will predominantly come down to whether third parties truly considered the parties to be married, as opposed to any suggestion that they simply ought to be considered as such.

In *Ackerman v Blackburn*[3] Miss Ackerman, the pursuer, sought a declarator that she had been married to Mr Logan. They had cohabited for just shy of four years. The cohabitation commenced in May 1994 and ceased in April 1998. Miss Ackerman raised her action after Mr Logan had passed away in a hillwalking accident. She also sought an interdict to prevent Mr Logan's executors (Blackburn and Logan), from intromitting with Mr Logan's estate until her action had been determined. The case was heard at the Court of

---

2   Family Law (Scotland) Act 2006, 2006, asp 2, section 3 (2)

3   *Ackerman v Blackburn* 2000 Fam L.R. 35

Session before Lord Nimmo Smith. Evidence was led to the effect that the parties had become engaged to be married in March 2006. Mr Logan had at that time purchased a ring for the pursuer. Miss Ackerman's position was that they subsequently went on what they considered to be their "honeymoon", staying in a hotel overnight and having a champagne dinner. She stated in evidence that thereafter they considered themselves to be married. This was contradicted by the defenders, who considered that Miss Ackerman and Mr Logan had been engaged to be married but were not in fact widely considered to be married. It was held that in order to establish marriage by cohabitation with habit and repute, it was necessary that there be both a mental element (consent to marry) and a factual element (either a cohabitation with habit and repute or some form of marriage ceremony). It was established in the *Ackerman* case that on the evidence there had been a future intention to marry, rather than the relationship *being* a marriage. Miss Ackerman appealed to the Inner House of the Court of Session on the basis that the Lord Ordinary had erred in making a finding that there had been insufficient evidence to support her position. The appeal was refused. The Inner House held that *"there had to be evidence that the habit and repute was so widespread as to leave no substantial doubt"*[4]. Establishing both a mental and factual element is not without its difficulties, which suggests that it is only worth going down this route if there is a very clear body of reliable evidence available to support the position.

An interesting example can be taken from the English case of *A v A*[5]. In *A v A* declarator of marriage was granted in circumstances where parties had believed themselves to be married. They had failed to give notice of the marriage prior to the ceremony taking place. They were then married in a mosque. They had taken advice from the

---

4   *Ackerman v Blackburn (No 1) 2002 SLT 37*
5   *A v A* [2013] 2 W.L.R. 606

Imam who conducted the ceremony prior to going ahead, although it later transpired that not only had appropriate notice not been given, but that the Imam was also not registered to carry out valid ceremonies. The parties, however, had believed themselves whole-heartedly to be married and had continued about their lives on that basis. Their friends and family all believed them to be married. This is exactly the type of situation where marriage by cohabitation with habit and repute might well be recognised under Scots law. It was held in *A v A* that the marriage could be held to be valid under English Law. Importantly in that case, both parties to the marriage wished to have the marriage legally recognised. It is acknowledged that the ease of establishing the mental element necessary to establish marriage by cohabitation with habit and repute is rather more difficult where parties are in dispute.

Subsection 3 and 4 Exception: Ceremonies Conducted Overseas

It is not the case that parties commencing their cohabitation post 4 May 2006 are unable to raise an action for declarator of marriage by cohabitation with habit and repute in all cases. A narrow but significant exception remains. If parties have entered into a marriage overseas which they believe to be valid, but discover following the death of one of the parties to the marriage that the marriage did not in fact have validity, marriage by cohabitation with habit and repute may still be established where the parties are (or were, at the time of death) both Scottish domiciled. This is set out in subsections (3) and (4) as follows:

> *"3(3) Nothing in subsection (1) shall affect the application of the rule in relation to cohabitation with habit and repute where –*
>
> (a) *the cohabitation with habit and repute began after commencement; and*

(b) *the conditions in subsection (4) are met.*

3(4) Those conditions are –

(a) *That the cohabitation with habit and repute was between two persons, one of whom, ("A"), is domiciled in Scotland;*

(b) *That the person with whom A was cohabiting, ("B"), died domiciled in Scotland;*

(c) *That, before the cohabitation with habit and repute began, A and B purported to enter into a marriage ('the purported marriage') outwith the United Kingdom;*

(d) *That, in consequence of the purported marriage, A and B believed themselves to be married to each other and continued in that belief until B's death;*

(e) *That the purported marriage was invalid under the law of the place where the purported marriage was entered into; and*

(f) *That A became aware of the invalidity of the purported marriage only after B's death.[6]"*

Proving such a case is likely to be difficult in the face of resistance from executors, given the emphasis placed on the belief held by the parties.

For the vast majority of clients entering a solicitor's office in Scotland and seeking legal advice on the claims available to cohabitants, if cohabitation either began after 4 May 2006; *or* it began prior to 4 May 2006 but third parties did <u>not</u> believe the parties to

---

6   Family Law (Scotland) Act 2006, 2006, asp 2, section 3 (3) and 3 (4)

be married, the provisions found in sections 25 to 29 of the 2006 Act will apply.

CHAPTER TWO
DEFINING COHABITATION

Cohabitant

In order to explore the options available to cohabitants under the 2006 Act, it is first necessary to define "cohabitant". This chapter explores the definition which is laid out in section 25 of the 2006 Act.

"Cohabitant" is defined in section 25 of the 2006 Act, as follows:

(1) *"… either member of a couple consisting of –*

    (a) *a man and a woman who are (or were) living together as if they were husband and wife; or*

    (b) *two persons of the same sex who are (or were) living together as if they were civil partners."*

The definition was revised by section 4 of the Marriage and Civil Partnership (Scotland) Act 2014 to define cohabitants as persons living together as though they are married. Those in platonic relationships, living together but not forming part of a couple, are not considered to be cohabitants for the purposes of the 2006 Act. Whilst it is clear that those who are merely flat mates may not apply, where is the line drawn? What of those who perceive themselves as a couple but are no longer engaged in a sexual relationship? What of those who live together as a couple but do not share rooms, banking arrangements, or socialise together with particular frequency? In such cases, careful evidence will require to be obtained from third parties to ensure that the criteria for establishing a cohabiting relationship can be met.

There is also a question mark over those living in polyamorous relationships. Such relationships cannot be said to fall within the definition of a "couple", but might they be construed as forming several couples? One would have thought not, given the requirement for parties to be living together as though they are married. That being the case and polygamy not being permitted under Scots Law, it is unlikely that such an argument could be made.

Part of the difficulty with cohabitation is the lack of formalisation of the relationship. There is no clear starting point as there is in a marriage or civil partnership and accordingly no clear expression of intention to form a particular quality of relationship. Since the 2006 Act came into force, cohabitants can be eligible to make claims regardless of whether they are perceived by others to be married. The question of whether cohabitants ought to "opt in" to the 2006 Act regime by formalising their intention to cohabit is one query which has been raised by the Scottish Law Commission as part of their consultation[1]. It seems unlikely that such a concept would sprout wings. It is, after all, the purpose of the provision for making claims under the 2006 Act that those who have failed (or simply chosen not to) formalise their relationship ought to be protected. This is particularly true of cases where there is an imbalance of power in the relationship, with one party wishing to formalise matters and the other resisting.

Section 25(2) – Factors to Take Into Account To Establish Cohabitation

In the meantime, the 2006 Act offers some further guidance. In terms of subsection (2) of section 25, the court is directed to have regard to:

---

1   Scottish Law Commission Report, "Aspects of Family Law", February 2020

(a) *the length of the period during which A and B have been living together (or lived together);*

(b) *the nature of their relationship during that period; and*

(c) *the nature and extent of any financial arrangements subsisting, or which subsisted, during that period.*

Gutcher v Butcher

The question of whether a relationship constituted a cohabiting one was examined in the case of *Gutcher v Butcher*[2] which was appealed to the Sheriff Principal in 2014. Much weight was attached in this case to the nature of the financial arrangements between the parties. Miss Gutcher, the pursuer at proof, was from Orkney. The defender hailed from Sheffield. Mr Butcher had moved to Orkney in 2006 and bought a property nearby to Miss Gutcher's property in January 2007. Mr Butcher's property was then renovated for use as a bed and breakfast establishment. Miss Gutcher helped with the renovation project and thereafter assisted Mr Butcher in running the "B&B" business. Mr Butcher retained sole financial responsibility for the business. There were no joint finances. The relationship was an intimate one. Miss Gutcher regularly stayed overnight at Mr Butcher's property. They holidayed and socialised together. Mr Butcher proposed early on in the relationship but Miss Gutcher declined. A preliminary proof was heard at Kirkwall Sheriff Court, during which Mr Butcher went so far as to state that "*We were a couple apart from we hadn't signed a piece of paper and we hadn't got rings on our fingers.*"[3] The Sheriff at first instance found that what he

---

2 *Gutcher v Butcher 2014 WL 4954935*

3 *Gutcher v Butcher, 2014 WL 4954935, para 11 (from proof transcript)*

described as *"critical parts"* of their relationship were kept separate, these being:

(1) The fact that Miss Gutcher retained her own separate property and continued to pay Council Tax there;

(2) Miss Gutcher told employers her home address was at the property she owned in her sole name;

(3) There was no joining of the parties' finances; and

(4) She had refused Mr Butcher's marriage proposal.[4]

The Sheriff found that the relationship was not a cohabiting one. His decision was appealed to Sheriff Principal Pyle, whose judgment was issued in 2014. The Sheriff Principal was scathing of both parties' pleadings and indicated that as a result the Sheriff had had a difficult task. Counsel for the appellant referred to, amongst other things, the fact that at proof the respondent (Mr Butcher) had said that he "lived with" the appellant (Miss Gutcher); the respondent said that he did the cooking and food shopping; that he did the appellant's ironing; that he gave her son lifts and that she had been to his parents' home on two occasions for Christmas. Criticism was also made of the Sheriff's reliance on the parties' finances not having been joined. The Sheriff Principal, whilst sympathetic to that position, did not consider that the Sheriff had erred in the exercise of his discretion and the appeal was refused. The Sheriff Principal noted that in order to constitute cohabitation:

> *"the living must have the characteristics of a married couple. But it is also true that such characteristics will change over time to reflect modern habits and ways of life."*[5]

---

4 All set out at para 7 of Sheriff Principal Pyle's judgement (citation above)

5 *Gutcher v Butcher 2014 WL 4954935, para 13*

He acknowledged that the absence or otherwise of sexual relationships would be a less significant factor than they might have been in the 1940s.

Perhaps Miss Gutcher may have had an easier task had the parties been living under the same roof, rather than Miss Gutcher splitting her time between the two homes. This case highlights the importance of examining each part of the parties' lives together if there is any doubt that the hurdle of establishing that there *was* a cohabitation may be cleared.

Length of Cohabitation

A claim may be made under the 2006 Act regardless of the length of the cohabitation, provided that the court can be satisfied that "cohabitation" has been established. There is no minimum period. This contrasts with a number of other jurisdictions and there has been much discussion as to whether a minimum time period ought to be introduced. It is generally accepted that those who cohabit for a longer period are more likely to intertwine their lives and their finances. However, the introduction of a time limit could prevent what would otherwise be perfectly stateable claims from being made. It may also lead to parties becoming prejudiced where they are brutally dumped just before the expiry of a cohabitation time limit.

Harley v Thompson

This was examined in *Harley v Thompson*[6], which came before Sheriff Hammond at Livingston Sheriff Court in 2015. The parties had commenced their cohabitation on 1 April 2011 and lived

---

6 *Harley v Thompson 2015 Fam L.R. 45*

(together with their children from prior relationships) together until 30 April 2012. They had therefore cohabited for little over a year. During the cohabitation the pursuer was the main breadwinner. The parties each owned their own properties prior to meeting. They purchased a property together in joint names, the deposit and fees for which were funded by the pursuer. The pursuer made various other financial contributions prior to and during the relationship, including repaying some of the defender's debts. She made a claim for a capital sum on separation. The defender's position was that the relationship had not been long enough to qualify as a cohabitation, although he did make certain financial concessions. Sheriff Hammond noted in his judgement that the legislation specifies no minimum period of cohabitation:

> "*The question is therefore to be answered by looking at the circumstances of the relationship as a whole; the duration of the cohabitation being a factor to be considered.... I am unable to dismiss their relationship as one of short term cohabitation undeserving of protection under the legislation.*"[7]

In making this assessment the Sheriff referred in particular to the fact that the parties had intended to live, together with the children, in a house which they had purchased jointly and with pooled expenditure, an arrangement which might, had it been successful, have been capable of subsisting for some prolonged period, as indeed had been the parties' intention.

Douglas v Bell

What might be made of a scenario where there have been two distinct periods of cohabitation, separated by a gap? This was the

---

7   *Paras 42, 43*

position in *Douglas v Bell*[8] which came before Sheriff MacFadyen at Hamilton Sheriff Court for debate on the issue of time-bar and the relevancy of the pursuer's pleadings. The pursuer was making a claim for a capital sum of £75,000 under section 28 of the 2006 Act. Her position was that she and Mr Bell had been in a relationship from 1984 to 2010. They had cohabited between January 2003 and May 2008 and again from December 2009 to June 2010 but had remained a couple during the time that they were not living together. The defender disputed that there had been any resumption of cohabitation. If he was correct about that, then his position was that the pursuer's claim must be time-barred, her action only having been raised in 2011, over one year after the parties had separated. Any claim, he contended, ought therefore to be restricted to the period from December 2009 to June 2010, if indeed cohabitation during that period were established. He also struck at the relevancy of the Pursuer's averments as to events occurring between the two purported cohabitation periods. As it was accepted by both parties that they had not been living together between May 2008 and December 2009, his position was that pleadings relating to that period were irrelevant and ought not to be admitted to proof. Counsel for the pursuer indicated that the defender's view of matters was too restrictive and that the court was:

> "*entitled to consider all of the facts and circumstances of the parties' relationship as a whole ..... if the Defender was correct then the court would have to ignore a period of cohabitation between the parties of five years, disregarding issues which may be relevant and proceed only on the basis of a false snapshot between December 2009 and June 2010*".[9]

---

8   *Douglas v Bell 2014 Fam L.R. 2*

9   Para 21

The Sheriff agreed with that approach. In relation to the time-bar issue, the Sheriff agreed that it was necessary to have a proof on the facts to determine whether the parties had indeed resumed living together from June 2009. It was not possible to ascertain whether the action was time-barred in the absence of such evidence. The Sheriff also disagreed with the Defender's contention that pleadings pertaining to what happened in the period prior to December 2009 were irrelevant, stating that:

"*I can see no logic in limiting the basis for assessment of the amount of any award of a capital sum to events during the most recent period of cohabitation. Such an approach would fly in the face of normal human experience.*"[10]

The defender's position that a claim ought to have been raised within one year of May 2008 when they ceased to cohabit was said to be "absurd" in circumstances where the parties continued to be in an intimate relationship throughout that period. However, it is clear that the action would have been time-barred had the cohabitation not resumed.

Interaction With Marriage/Civil Partnership

The phrasing of the legislation as it stands allows parties to be married or civil partnered with one person and cohabiting with another simultaneously, either where they are separated from their spouse/civil partner and cohabiting full time with the cohabitant, or living in a "double life" scenario, appearing to live with each person. Being married or civil partnered to another person will not prevent a 2006 Act claim from being made.

---

10 Para 42

CHAPTER THREE
JURISDICTION

Having defined cohabitation, it is necessary to give thought to the implications of where (geographically speaking) the parties cohabited together. On reaching the stage of ascertaining that your client has indeed been in a cohabiting relationship, the jurisdictional rules need to be examined – does Scots Law apply?

If both parties to a cohabiting relationship are Scottish born and bred, with a future intention to remain in Scotland and they cohabited in Scotland for the duration of their cohabiting relationship, the answer is straightforward – Scot Law applies. However, 2006 Act claims can be made in certain circumstances even where the cohabitation took place out with Scotland.

Claims on Separation ("Section 28 Claims")

Section 28 claims can be raised in a court which would have jurisdiction to deal with the parties' divorce or dissolution had the parties been married or civil partnered. This is set out at section 28 (9) (a) and (b). Jurisdiction for opposite sex married couples currently follows *Brussels II Revised* and is enshrined in the provisions of the Domicile and Matrimonial Proceedings Act 1973 and extended to same sex married couples by virtue of the (Marriage (Same Sex Couples) (Jurisdictions and Recognition of Judgements) (Scotland) Regulations 2014, such that Scottish courts have jurisdiction where any of the following apply:

- Both spouses are habitually resident in Scotland;

- Both spouses were last habitually resident in Scotland and one still resides there;

- The defender is habitually resident in Scotland;

- The pursuer is habitually resident in Scotland and has resided there for at least a year before the action was raised;

- The pursuer is habitually resident in Scotland and has resided there for at least 6 months before the action was raised and is either a national of an EU Member State or (for UK and Ireland) is domiciled in Scotland;

- Both spouses are domiciled in Scotland.

If none of the above apply, the action can be raised based on the domicile of one party to the action at the time at which the action is raised.

Accordingly, a section 28 claim may be raised in circumstances where the cohabitation itself did not take place in Scotland. Likewise, parties who have cohabited in Scotland may be unable to make a claim under Scots Law in circumstances where they cannot meet the criteria to establish Scottish habitual residence or Scottish domicile.

Claims on Death ("Section 29 Claims")

The appropriate court for making a section 29 claim is noted at section 29 (5):

"*(5) An application under this section may be made to—*

(a) the Court of Session;

(b) a sheriff in the sheriffdom in which the deceased was habitually resident at the date of death;

(c) if at the date of death it is uncertain in which sheriffdom the deceased was habitually resident, the sheriff at Edinburgh."

In order to make a section 29 claim, the deceased <u>must</u> have been Scottish domiciled at the date of death and living with their cohabitant, by virtue of section 29 (1) (b).

Chebotareva v Khandro

The question of jurisdiction was examined in the case of *Chebotareva v Khandro (King's Executrix)[1]* which came before Sheriff Ward at Stirling Sheriff Court, who issued judgement in March 2008. The applicant, Miss Chebotareva, made a claim against the estate of her deceased cohabitee, Mr King, seeking the transfer of Mr King's interest in a property in Stirling to her and/or a capital sum payment. She contended that she and Mr King had been habitually resident in Stirling, having cohabited there together until the date of Mr King's death and that he was domiciled in Scotland. In particular, she stated that she and Mr King had lived in the property owned by him (for which she sought the transfer) from July 2005 until he died in May 2006. The action was opposed by Mr King's sister, the executrix, who argued that Mr King was neither habitually resident in Stirling, nor domiciled in Scotland. In relation to residence, the defender argued that Mr King did not live in Stirling. The Sheriff appointed the case to a proof before answer, at which

---

1   *Chebotareva v Khando (King's Executrix) 2008 Fam. L.R. 66*

evidence for the defender was led to the effect that Mr King had food in his London property suggestive of it being occupied; he claimed jobseeker's allowance in London and visited the job centre in London fortnightly; he leased a workshop in London; he was registered to vote in London; in 2004 he had told an immigration official that he and the pursuer lived together in London; very little electricity was used in the Stirling property; the bins were never put out; Mr King was rarely seen by the downstairs neighbour in Stirling and Mr King had told the Council that the Stirling property was unoccupied in order to receive a Council Tax rebate. The pursuer contended that she did live in the Stirling property with Mr King, but that they rarely went out, used little electricity and visited London frequently. The Sheriff did not accept her evidence as credible and found that Mr King had not been habitually resident in Stirling. The Sheriff also refused to accept that the deceased had been Scottish domiciled. The deceased had been born in London, died in London and maintained his London connections. Accordingly he had retained his domicile of origin. The Sheriff stated that "any expressions of intent [to become Scottish domiciled] were never translated into an action which showed disavowal of his domicile of origin".[2]

Accordingly, the action was dismissed for want of jurisdiction. Careful evidence will therefore require to be led by applicants, particularly in cases where there may be hostile executors keen to ensure that section 29 claims do not bear fruit.

---

2   Para 14

CHAPTER FOUR
RIGHTS OF COHABITANTS

This chapter takes a brief look at the rights which cohabitants have by virtue of the cohabitation.

Rights In Household Goods

Section 26 of the 2006 Act provides a presumption that each party to a cohabitation has an <u>equal</u> right to share in household goods acquired during the cohabitation. This presumption is rebuttable. Gifts and inheritances are expressly excluded from this presumption[1] and so will remain the property of the recipient. Those in cohabiting relationships would be well advised to keep detailed paper trails on receipt of such assets, or of any assets purchased by them individually, in case of any disagreement down the line.

"Household goods" is stated to include any goods kept or used "at any time during the cohabitation in any residence"[2] in which the parties cohabit(ed). Money, securities, motor vehicles and pets are expressly excluded. Again, keeping a paper trail can be important to avoid ambiguity about these matters, although one might expect that only family lawyers might be cynical enough to do so.

---

1   Family Law (Scotland) Act 2006, 2006 asp 2, section 26 (2)
2   Section 26 (4)

Jackson v Burns

In *Jackson v Burns*[3], the pursuer sought a capital sum payment under section 28. In addition, he sought delivery of certain household goods, which failing a further capital sum payment of £1,000 to account for his share of the expenditure he had made to assist the defender in acquiring those goods. In his judgment the Sheriff determined that to make an order for delivery he would have needed to be satisfied that *"certain specified and sufficiently identified items had been retained by the Defender and were the sole property of the Pursuer."*[4] However, the evidence was that the pursuer had contributed 50% of the cost of a handful of items. All other items in the property in which the parties cohabited for a period of eleven years had been purchased by the defender and retained, following separation, by her. Notably, the Sheriff took issue with the fact that two separate section 28(a) claims were pled within the same action, doubting that such a course would be permitted where the legislation expressly provides for the making of "an order" for a capital sum payment. However, the Sheriff also considered that no sufficient evidence had been led to allow him to properly value the disadvantage to the pursuer in no longer being able to use those household goods to which he had contributed. In any event, recognition was given to the fact that the benefit the pursuer had received of living in a fully furnished property for eleven years would likely dwarf any disadvantage said to be suffered under that heading.[5]

What might sensibly be taken from this is that paper trails are useful. Although subsequent case law has put it beyond doubt that parties are not expected to have embarked on an accounting exercise during or after their relationship, bank statements and receipts can be useful

---

3   *Jackson v Burns 2019 Fam. L.R. 88*
4   Para 69
5   See paras 68 to 78

if there is any dispute down the line and so certainly (for transactions involving valuable assets, at least) ought to be encouraged. It should also be borne in mind (and highlighted to clients) that the value of any claims for delivery of household goods is likely to be outweighed significantly by the costs of litigating. Family law clients ought to be encouraged to focus on their likely final net outcome, <u>including</u> money to be spent on solicitors' fees and the risks of awards of expenses being made against them, rather than fighting matters on principle.

Rights in Certain Money and Property

Section 27 of the 2006 Act provides that, in the absence of any agreement to the contrary, any money or property deriving from an allowance given by one cohabitant for joint household expenses shall belong to each cohabitant in equal shares. Equally, any property acquired out of such money shall belong to the parties in equal shares. This expressly <u>excludes</u> a property bought as the parties' main residence in which they live or lived together.

Occupancy Rights

The occupancy rights of cohabitants is regulated by section 18 of the Matrimonial Homes (Family Protection) (Scotland) Act 1981. Unlike married or civil partnered parties, those who are cohabiting do <u>not</u> have automatic occupancy rights to live in property owned or rented in the name of their cohabitee. However, a court may grant occupancy rights to the "non entitled" cohabitant for a period of six months. This period can be extended for a further period or periods, "no such period exceeding 6 months". These provisions prevent a cohabitant from being left high and dry and often go hand in hand with protective orders, as explored below.

Protective Orders

Cohabitants have access to "domestic interdicts" by virtue of section 18A of the Matrimonial Homes (Family Protection) (Scotland) Act 1981, which was inserted when the 2006 Act was enacted. In terms of section 18A, cohabitants can apply for interdicts to protect them, or any child in their care, from specified conduct of the defender; or to prohibit the defender from entering or remaining in the family home (an "exclusion order"); any other residence owned by the pursuer; the pursuer's place of work; and any school attended by a child in the pursuer's care. These interdicts can be granted on a permanent or interim basis. Powers of arrest may be attached to such interdicts by virtue of the provisions of the Protection from Abuse (Scotland) Act 2001.

CHAPTER FIVE
SECTION 28 – DEFINING SEPARATION

Section 28 claims are made on the separation of a previously cohabiting couple, or as the legislation would have it *"where cohabitants cease to cohabit otherwise than by reason of the death of one (or both) of them"*.[1] By far the majority of reported 2006 Act cases concern this section. We deal first with the issue of the date of separation.

Defining "Separation"

It makes some sense to start with a look at how "separation" can be defined (and if necessary, evidenced). Very rarely do parties put down a marker as to separation in the form of an angry email (although this does happen!) and so this would seem to be predominantly fact based. As with marriage, parties may be separated insofar as they are no longer living together as spouses, whilst still being under the same roof. No specific provision is provided on the definition of separation and so in the absence thereof, there are some sensible practical steps which can be taken:

1. In the event of a party entering your office in circumstances where a section 28 claim appears justified, it is good advice to write to the other party setting out specifically the date at which the separation occurred. In the absence of any other evidence, this may be persuasive.

2. For those who have the good fortune or good sense to enter into pre cohabitation agreements, provision ought to be made

---

1   Section 28 (1)

therein as to how the fact of the separation will be determined. It is common in such agreements to indicate that the separation must be signified in writing (email being acceptable) by one party to the other.

Where there is a dispute as to the date of separation, the court is likely to adopt an approach similar to that taken where marriage/civil partnership comes to an end, resting the evidence on no one single factor, but on a range of factors. This might include separation of sleeping arrangements, changes to financial arrangements, the physical vacation of the property by one of the parties and crucially the awareness or otherwise of family and friends.

Fairley v Fairley

The date of separation was hotly contested in the case of *Fairley v Fairley*[2] which went to proof at the Court of Session (Outer House). In that case, the pursuer contended that the separation had taken place in June 2006, whilst the defender's position was that he had left for good in April 2006. This was significant, of course, as had the defender's position been established there could not have been any award made under the 2006 Act, which does not have retrospective effect. Lord McEwan preferred the evidence of the pursuer, noting that this was not a legal question, but one of "credibility and reliability"[3]. A decision was made in favour of the pursuer, who had been able to provide clear evidence and consistency of dates, corroborated by nine witnesses. Much use was made of anchoring the chronology of dates provided by the pursuer to important seasonal events or events significant to the witnesses, including whether or not it was

---

2   *Fairley v Fairley* 2008 Fam. L.R. 112

3   Para 3

daylight, family birthdays, the death of a relative, the start of the football World Cup and so on – a useful technique for any litigator.

M v T

The date of separation was also contested in the Aberdeen Sheriff Court case of *M v T*[4] which went to preliminary proof on the matter in 2011 before Sheriff Bovey. Sheriff Bovey's judgment contains a noteworthy observation at paragraphs 27-30 as to the significance of awareness of third parties, as follows:

> " 27. *Is the presentation of the parties as a couple relevant as a factor in deciding whether they are to be regarded as cohabiting? Does the presentation of the parties as a couple colour the consideration of the indicators as to cohabitation?*
>
> 28. *The issue may have particular relevance in this case as I accept [M's] evidence that he would not have continued to work for free on the defender's house if he had not believed that she and his father were still partners. He put it crisply: "They couldn't have separated in 2009 or all these social events and work wouldn't have happened."*
>
> 29. *This is, of course, not correct: the parties could maintain a pretence of cohabitation for an ulterior motive such as not upsetting the family, having domestic renovation completed or in the hope of reconciliation.*
>
> 30. *But given the public nature of the institution of marriage which underpins the issue I have to decide, I am inclined to answer both questions in the affirmative.* "

---

4   *M v T* [2011] 11 WLUK 503

B v B

If one party moves out, is there an automatic assumption that the cohabitation has come to an end? That question was considered in *B v B*[5]. In that case, the parties had been cohabiting for around 23 years. The defender argued that the action was time barred, contending that the cohabitation had ceased when he had left the home in which the parties lived together and moved into a new property in December 2010. If that were true, then the pursuer's claim for a capital sum of £100,000 had not been raised within a one year period following separation and would be time barred. The pursuer contended that the cohabitation had not come to an end until June 2011 and that her claim had therefore been brought in time. The defender was hanging his hat on the fact that he had, in December 2010, moved into another property. However, the Sheriff heard evidence to the effect that following that date the defender continued to refer to the pursuer as his wife, would say that he lived with her, continued to share in bills such as car insurance and that the parties occasionally socialised together. The defender had left various belongings at the house he had shared with the pursuer, had retained a key and visited regularly. The Sheriff found that the pursuer's claim was not time barred. The defender appealed to Sheriff Principal Stephen. The defender's main position at appeal was that the Sheriff, having found that the defender had physically moved out of the property, ought to have found that the cohabitation had ceased at that point and that the case was time barred. The Sheriff Principal refused the appeal. She found that *"in my view, undue concentration on the words "living together" is both wrong in law and inequitable... [and] ignores the realities of life."*[6]

---

5   *B v B* 2014 WL 4636823
6   *B v B, 2014 WL 4636823*

Whilst it is not suggested that a 2006 Act claim would get off the ground where parties are no longer under the same roof <u>at all</u>, the observations made in this case tend to suggest that it is not necessary for parties to spend 365 days a year living in the same building. Common examples of parties cohabiting together but not always being under the same roof would include those in the oil industry working on rotation; or a situation where one party spends a period of time in hospital.

Defining the date of separation is crucially important in section 28 claims due to time bar, which is considered further in Chapter 6.

CHAPTER SIX
SECTION 28 – TIME BAR

Time Limit

If you remember no other advice from this book, remember this: a section 28 claim **must** be raised "not later than one year after the day on which the parties cease to cohabit". There is authority to suggest that lodging an Initial Writ with the court may be sufficient in terms of "raising" an action (see *Secretary of State for Trade and Industry v Josolyne[1]*); however, this has been challenged and to be absolutely safe it is best to have an action lodged, warranted and successfully served in advance of the time limit expiring. Equally, if you are anticipating making a counter claim for your client in reliance on the other party's solicitor confirming that an action will shortly be raised, do not wait for them to get their action in. If you are getting close to the line, you are better to get a separate action up and running for your client than to "miss the boat" and be unable to present your client's counter claim.

Time Limits – Discretion?

As the law stands, the court has absolutely no discretion to extend the time limit for making a section 28 claim. Equally, agents cannot currently agree to extend the time limit so as to avoid incurring the cost of litigation. Both of these points are subjects of the SLC consultation. Identification of the date of separation is therefore vitally important, as explored in Chapter 5.

---

1   *Secretary of State for Trade and Industry v Josolyne, 1990 SLT (Sh Ct) 48*

Whilst providing former cohabitants with the certainty of knowing that they are safe from any claim (and therefore free to cohabit with someone else without fear of leaving themselves exposed to multiple section 28 claims), this rule gives cohabitants precious little time to accept the end of the relationship, consult a solicitor and enter into any meaningful negotiation. A lack of education in relation to the rights available to cohabiting couples is a real obstacle for practitioners and it is not uncommon for clients to reach out for legal advice once the time limit has already expired. In that event, there may still be a remedy available under the law of unjustified enrichment: see Chapter 13.

Lawley v Sutton

It is important not only to ensure that you have made any necessary claims, but also to ensure that your written pleadings are in good shape with a view to preventing challenge. The importance of pleading your case well cannot be overstated. In *Lawley v Sutton*[2] the defender sought to introduce a Minute of Amendment. Part 1 of the Minute of Amendment was to introduce a section 28 counter claim and a crave for division and sale. Counsel for the pursuer submitted that that part of the amendment should not be allowed. A counter-claim was time barred, it being more than a year after the parties had ceased to cohabit. When the defences had been lodged the position regarding counter claim was not in the correct form. Counsel for the defender stated that the defender's counter claim had been contained within the body of the defences. This was simply a matter of structuring. The Sheriff allowed the amendment in full, finding that all of the points to be made had already been clear within the body of the defences, despite the fact that no section 28 crave had been made.

---

2 *Lawley v Sutton [2010] 3 WLUK 501*

There would not, of course, have been such a finding had the required level of detail not been provided in the pleadings to date.

Simpson v Downie

This issue was also explored in the case of *Simpson v Downie*[3] in which Mr Simpson sought a capital sum payment under section 28 from his former cohabitee, Miss Downie. The solicitors for the Defender, Miss Downie, lodged defences in which she sought to introduce a claim of her own against Mr Simpson. However, the defences were lodged after the one-year time limit had expired. A debate was therefore held to ascertain whether the claim in her defences could proceed. The Sheriff at first instance determined that her claim could proceed, indicating that the claim she made formed an integral part of her defences and was also relevant to any further argument about off-setting. An appeal to the Sheriff Principal was unsuccessful. However, a further appeal to the Inner House was sustained, with it being determined that the statutory time limit was absolute and there could be no room for discretion:

> *"No doubt a strict statutory régime of this kind may work [sic.] hardship in some cases, for example where one party delays making a claim until the one year period is nearly up and the other, taken by surprise, is left with no opportunity to follow suit. On the other hand, Parliament must have envisaged such circumstances when the relevant provisions were enacted, and deliberately elected to make no provision for discretionary relief."*[4]

---

3   *Simpson v Downie* 2013 SLT 178 CSIH
4   Para 14

Garrad v Inglis

The issue of time bar was also considered in *Garrad v Inglis*[5], in which the Sheriff considered the question of whether the parties were still cohabiting and found that the matter was time barred. In reaching that view, the Sheriff considered that the following factors ought to be taken into account in determining whether the parties were cohabiting:

> "9. In my opinion, various factors to be considered in answering that question, which will include: (1) the length of time during which the parties lived together, (2) the amount and nature of the time the parties spent together, (3) whether they lived under the same roof in the same household, (4) whether they slept together, (5) whether they had sexual intercourse, (6) whether they ate together, (7) whether they had a social life together, (8) whether they supported each other, talked to and were affectionate to each other, (9) outward appearances, (10) their financial arrangements, whether they shared resources, household and child-care tasks, (11) the intentions of each party and whether any of them were communicated to the other party, and (12) physical separation. None of the factors is conclusive on its own."[6]

McIntyre v Stewart

What if a section 28 claim is split into different component parts, some of which are raised timeously whilst others are not? This was considered in the Haddington Sheriff Court case of *McIntyre v Stewart*[7]. In this action, the pursuer claimed a capital sum of £340,000 in terms of section 28 (2) (a) of the 2006 Act. Shortly

---

5   *Garras v Inglis* 2013 WL 6980541

6   Para. 9

7   *McIntyre v Stewart* 2014 Fam LR 7

before proof, she sought to amend her pleadings to add in a new crave for £50,000 in terms of section 28 (2) (b) (economic burden of childcare). This was opposed by the defender, who argued that the court did not have jurisdiction to entertain what was, he contended, essentially a new claim given that a year had elapsed from the date of the parties' separation. In allowing the amendment to the pursuer's pleadings, Sheriff Braid held that the defender's reading of the legislation was too narrow and that once a section 28 claim is lodged, the whole terms of section 28 are engaged.

Time Bar: Advice for Clients

There are three points arising from this which are relevant when advising clients.

1. Sometimes the right legal advice for your client may be to do nothing and to rely on the fact that their former cohabitee will either be too slow to raise a claim, or lack the awareness to do so. However morally dubious this may seem, this can prove to be extremely cost-effective advice.

2. If you are involved in negotiations with another agent or with a party litigant and things appear to be stalling, get your action lodged, warranted and served with plenty of time to spare. It is far better to raise an action timeously and sist it (put it on hold) at an early stage for negotiation to take place than to risk leaving your client exposed. Although some cost will be incurred with this approach, this will also have the added benefit of putting a firework under negotiations and incentivising parties to think constructively.

3. If you are unexpectedly served with an action in the final hour, you may not have time to competently make a counter claim.

However, you can still present the reasons why any claim made by the pursuer has been offset during the period of the parties' cohabitation (see Chapter 8).

CHAPTER SEVEN
SECTION 28 – WHAT ORDERS CAN THE COURT MAKE?

Clients may assume that if they can establish that they have indeed been cohabiting, they can apply for orders akin to those available to couples who are married or in a civil partnership. This chapter considers which orders can competently be sought. It should be borne in mind, in considering this, that the presumption at the end of a marriage or civil partnership is that property will be shared fairly between the parties. The presumption at the cessation of cohabitation is that the parties will each retain their own property – see Sheriff Hendry's comments in *F v D*[1].

Section 28 (2) – Possible Orders

In terms of section 28 (2), the court has the authority to make any of the following orders:

(a) An order for payment of a capital sum;

(b) An order requiring the defender to pay an amount in respect of the economic burden of caring, post separation, for a child of whom the cohabitants are parents; and

(c) "Such interim order as it thinks fit".

---

1 *F v D* 2009 Fam. L.R. 111, para 7.

The court may order that any capital sum payment may be made by instalments rather than as a lump figure[2]. By far the vast majority of the case law concerns claims made under section 28 (2) (a).

The court <u>cannot</u>, in satisfaction of a section 28 claim, make a final order for any of the following:

- Payments of aliment or periodical allowance (although aliment may be claimed separately under the Family Law (Scotland) Act 1985 by a parent on behalf of a child in certain circumstances);

- The transfer of property; or

- The sharing of a pension.

The above orders would all be available to parties to marriages/civil partnerships on divorce/dissolution. The lack of the ability to transfer a property is a source of concern for many clients, particularly where parties have cohabited in a property owned by one of them for a lengthy period and the other party has suddenly to uplift themselves and build a new life. The sale of a property cannot be ordered either in terms of section 28 (although it may be possible to use an action of division and sale for this purpose where property is jointly owned). The reality in any event is that a property may sometimes need to be sold to satisfy any order for a capital sum payment which the court may make. It is competent to crave a section 28 order and an action for division and sale within the same action (see *Lawley v Sutton[3]*).

---

2   Section 28 (7)
3   *Lawley v Sutton* [2010] 3 WLUK 501

CHAPTER EIGHT
SECTION 28 – ECONOMIC ADVANTAGE AND ECONOMIC DISADVANTAGE

In order to make a successful claim under section 28, it is necessary for the applicant to show either that they have suffered an economic disadvantage in the interests of the defender or any "relevant child"; or that the defender has been economically advantaged as a result of contributions made by the pursuer and that there ought to be some financial compensation in order to achieve a fair outcome. This chapter looks at how such arguments might be addressed.

Evaluating Potential Claims: Steps to Consider

Having established that your client was in a cohabiting relationship and that the one year time limit for making a claim under section 28 has not expired, the process of evaluating claims should involve consideration of the following:

1. Has there been any economic advantage to the defender during the cohabitation?

2. Has there been any economic disadvantage suffered by the pursuer in the interests of the defender or any relevant child?

3. What contributions have been made by each party during the period of the cohabitation?

4. Have any of the advantages/disadvantages gained or suffered by one party been offset by disadvantages/advantages suffered or gained by the other?

5. How (on a broad bush basis) can any claims arising from the above be evidenced and quantified?

6. Is there some identifiable unfairness which has arisen as a result of the relationship which should be compensated for?

7. Consider the parties' resources.

Definitions

Economic advantage/disadvantage

In deciding whether a section 28 order is justified, the court is directed to have regard to:

> *"Whether (and, if so, to what extent) the defender has derived economic advantage from contributions made by the applicant; and whether (and, if so, to what extent) the applicant has suffered economic disadvantage in the interests of – (i) the defender; or (ii) any relevant child".*[1]

The Act defines "economic advantage" as <u>including</u> (although not being limited to) gains in capital, income and earning capacity[2]. The most common example of a gain in "income and earning capacity" would be one cohabitant staying at home to raise children, thereby affording the other to take steps to further their career without childcare restraints. Conversely, an example of an economic disad-

---

1   Section 28 (3)
2   Section 28 (9)

vantage might be that the party remaining at home with children has failed to progress their career, thereby impacting on their earning capacity and their ability to build their capital and pension interests.

It is not necessary to prove <u>both</u> that there has been economic advantage to the defender <u>and</u> economic disadvantage to the pursuer – see the comments of Sheriff Hendry in *F v D*.[3]

Relevant Child

A "relevant child" is a child of whom both cohabitants are parents, or a child who has been accepted by them as a child of the family.[4] As in divorce cases, this can occasionally (although rarely) be disputed.

Contribution

A "contribution" need not be a financial contribution. Whilst some cases are cut and dried (Bob gave Mary £20,000 and she used it to renovate a house in her sole name), others will involve taking a closer look at the quality of the relationship and each party's role therein. The Act expressly states that "contributions" includes indirect and non-financial contributions[5]. In particular, this includes "*any such contribution made by looking after any relevant child or any house in which they [the cohabitants] cohabited*" (section 28 (9)). The fact that this is so clearly stated brings home the fact that stay-at-home parents were certainly in mind when this legislation was formulated.

---

3 *F v D* 2009 Fam. L.R. 111, paragraphs 46 and 47
4 Section 28 (10)
5 Section 28 (9)

Selkirk v Chisholm

In *Selkirk v Chisholm*[6] the defender was assoilzied, the Sheriff finding that the pursuer's contributions (being primarily contributions to normal household bills and looking after the home) did not directly lead to the economic advantage said to be gained by the defender. However, later case law has established that there does not need to be a direct causal link between the contribution of one party and the economic advantage gained by the other – see *Gow v Grant* at page 48. This demonstrates the way in which the interpretation of section 28 claims has evolved since their inception.

Quantification

It is clear that the legislation, in directing the court to consider "to what extent" there has been any economic advantage or disadvantage, intends that there be some quantification of the parties' respective positions. There has been some discrepancy in case law as to how precisely the quantification needs to be carried out. Whilst it is now clear that an accounting exercise is neither envisaged nor appropriate, there will need to be some sufficiency of evidence to allow the court to determine the level of any award which might be made.

Jamieson v Rodhouse

It was established in *Jamieson v Rodhouse*[7] that although a broad-brush approach may be taken, an award cannot be made in circumstances where a claim simply cannot be quantified. In that case, the

---

6   *Selkirk v Chisholm* 2011 Fam L.R. 56

7   *Jamieson v Rodhouse* 2009 Fam. L.R. 34

pursuer had sought a capital sum in terms of section 28 of the Act following the parties' separation. The parties had cohabited for 31 years, always in homes owned by the defender. The pursuer's son lived with them. Throughout the cohabitation, the pursuer paid for most of the food for both parties and carried out housework. The defender paid for the household bills and the mortgage. No evidence was led to quantify the pursuer's contributions. Sheriff Hogg held that:

> *'the poverty of the evidence in this case leads me to conclude that the pursuer has only proved that the defender has derived economic advantage from contributions made by the pursuer but that only to the extent of indirect contributions of providing household cooking and cleaning services and direct contributions of payments for food. I am unable to place any financial value on these services and thus the economic advantage.'*[8]

Accordingly, no award was made and the defender was assoilzied. This may be too strict an approach to adopt in light of later case law.

F v D

The Kirkcaldy Sheriff Court case of *F v D* concerned parties who had cohabited from 2002 to May 2007. They lived together with the pursuer's son from a previous relationship and a child of their relationship together. The pursuer sought a capital sum payment in terms of section 28 (2) (a) and a sum under section 28 (2) (b) in respect of the burden for caring for the parties' child. During the cohabitation the pursuer had paid for household bills, clothing and groceries and cared for the parties' child (and her child from her previous relationship). She was a student and worked part time. The

---

8   Para. 42

defender, who began the cohabitation with £20,000 of debt and no assets, was able to purchase a property during the cohabitation, funded partly by a loan of £1,500 from the pursuer's father. At the end of the cohabitation his earnings had increased by around £6,000/year and he had achieved net sale proceeds of £28,441 from property. The Sheriff found that the defender had derived an economic advantage from the cohabitation and awarded a capital sum in relation to that element of the claim, as well as a further sum of £3,000 in respect of school uniform and childcare costs for the parties' child. There was no credible or reliable evidence as to any disadvantage suffered by him. The Sheriff considered that only a broad-brush approach could be applied as there was insufficient evidence to allow a thorough quantification to be carried out. Whilst it is not envisaged that a strict calculation should be carried out, this case emphasises the importance of providing the court with as much relevant information as possible. The pursuer would have been in a stronger position had she produced evidence as to her likely career trajectory and earning capacity had she not been inhibited in her career by caring for the parties' child.

Cameron v Leal

The issue of quantification and provision of sufficient evidence was again reflected upon in the Aberdeen Sheriff Court case of *Cameron v Leal*[9]. In this case, the defender had written off the pursuer's car due to drink driving during the period of the parties' cohabitation. The pursuer sought a total sum of £16,500, £12,500 of which she argued was due to the disadvantage suffered by her in respect of the written off vehicle. Following the car being written off, the parties took out a joint loan to repay the vehicle finance. The Sheriff found that the writing off of the vehicle represented an economic loss to

---

9   *Cameron v Leal* 2010 S.L.T (Sh Ct) 48

both parties and not simply to the pursuer. He also found that it was not possible to properly assess any economic disadvantage suffered by the pursuer, nor to carry out an off-setting exercise (see below) as no evidence had been provided as to the term of the loan nor the arrangements for repayment. In the circumstances, no award was made.

Whilst more recent case law (see *Gow v Grant*) tells us that strict quantification is unnecessary (particularly when assessing non-financial contributions), as with any case, the more material that can be provided to the court to substantiate a claim, the better.

Offsetting

Having assessed whether there has been any economic advantage to the defender as a result of the pursuer's contributions, the court is then directed to consider whether that advantage has been offset by any disadvantage suffered by the defender in the interest of the pursuer or any relevant child[10]. Equally, if the court finds that the pursuer has suffered a disadvantage in the interests of the defender or any relevant child, it must then consider whether this has been offset by any advantage the pursuer has derived from contributions by the defender.[11] Even where a defender does not wish to counter claim in a section 28 claim, it is therefore important to set out in some detail the way in which any advantage/disadvantage claimed by the applicant has been offset, with a view to heading off the applicant's claim.

---

10 Section 28 (5)

11 Section 28 (6)

Mitchell v Gibson

In *Mitchell v Gibson*[12] the Sheriff at first instance awarded a capital sum of £2,000 to the pursuer in terms of section 28 on the basis that prior to the cohabitation she had lived in accommodation of a good standard and at the end of the cohabitation she moved out of the defender's home and required to spend £2,000 to put her new rented accommodation into a good standard. The defender appealed the decision. The appeal was allowed and the defender absolved. The Sheriff Principal noted that:

> " *In terms of s.28 the court has to have regard firstly to the extent to which the defender has derived economic advantage from contributions made by the applicant (subs.(3)) and to offset against that any economic disadvantage suffered by the defender in the interests of the applicant (subs.(5)). Secondly the court has to have regard to any economic disadvantage suffered by the applicant in the interests of the defender (subs.(3)) and to offset against that any economic advantage the applicant has derived from contributions made by the defender. The approach of the legislature seems therefore to require separate assessment of the two matters referred to in subs.(3), so that in considering whether the defender has derived economic advantage from contributions made by the applicant it is not legitimate to offset economic advantage derived by the applicant from contributions made by the defender. In a similar vein, in considering whether the applicant has suffered economic disadvantage in the interests of the defender, it is not legitimate to offset against such disadvantage any economic disadvantage suffered by the defender in the interests of the applicant.* "[13]

---

12 *Mitchell v Gibson* 2011 Fam. L.R. 53

13 Para. 9

It is important to structure pleadings accurately and to ensure that these two issues are very clearly and separately stated to avoid falling into a technical trap. If offsetting is to be relied upon, this must be sufficiently pled if the court is expected to have any regard to it – see comments of Lady Smith in the Inner House appeal of *Melvin v Christie*[14].

Harley v Robertson

In *Harley v Robertson*[15] the pursuer sought a capital sum under section 28 as well as a claim for unjustified enrichment. The pursuer's section 28 claim relied heavily on the fact that she had expended funds on the defender's property; however, evidence was led to the effect that these were really commissioned for her benefit, having not been requested by the defender. Although the Sheriff was prepared to accept that the defender had gained an economic advantage of £2,000 in respect of the increase in value to his property as a result of the works, this was offset by the expenditure which had been incurred by the defender in favour of the pursuer throughout the cohabitation. The Sheriff noted that there should not be a bookkeeping exercise and that a broad axe approach was appropriate; however, some guidance as to ballpark figures could be taken by the evidence led on the defender's behalf.

See also *Cameron v Lukes*[16], in which the defender's pleadings and evidence were insufficient to allow an offsetting exercise to be properly carried out.

---

14 *Melvin v Christie* 2016 Fam. L.R. 116

15 *Harley v Robertson* 2011 WL 6329320

16 *Cameron v Lukes* [2013] 12 WLUK 22

Key Case on Section 28 (2) (a) : *Gow v Grant*

The key case we have on the interpretation of the 2006 Act is the Supreme Court decision in *Gow v Grant*[17]. In this case, Miss Gow (aged 64) and Mr Grant (58) met a singles club and commenced a relationship. Mr Grant asked Miss Gow to move into his house in Penicuik, which she did on the condition that the parties first became engaged. This they duly did. They cohabited together from 2003 to 2008.

During the cohabitation, Mr Grant encouraged Miss Gow to sell her flat (which she had owned prior to the cohabitation), which she did in 2003 for £50,000. She used some of those proceeds for herself and put the rest towards the parties' living expenses. Mr Grant retained his home (in which the parties lived together) throughout and continued to live in it post separation. Had Miss Gow retained her flat, it would have been worth £88,000 at the time of the proof.

In 2003, Mr Grant asked Miss Gow not to return to work when her contract ended. Miss Gow also made an unequal contribution to some timeshares which the parties purchased together.

Following separation, Miss Gow raised a claim under section 28. The Sheriff at first instance awarded her the sum of £39,500. This was to reflect the increase in value of her flat if she had retained it (£38,000) and £1,500 for the over payment she had made in respect of the timeshares.

On appeal, the Court of Session found that no capital sum payment was due.

---

17 2013 SC (UKSC) 1

Miss Gow appealed to the Supreme Court. The Supreme Court rein-stated the original award of £39,500. It was observed by Lady Hale that:

> "People do not keep such running accounts and the cost of working things out in detail is quite disproportionate to the task of doing justice between the parties. _Section 28(3)(a) and (9) of the Family Law (Scotland) Act 2006_ requires regard to be had to non-fin-ancial contributions; the economic disadvantage to which regard must be had under _sec 28(3)(b)_ must be suffered in the interests of the other, but does not have to amount even to a non-financial contribution. Who can say whether the non-financial contribu-tions, or the sacrifices, made by one party were offset by the board and lodging paid for by the other? That is not what living together in an intimate relationship is all about. It is much more prac-ticable to consider where they were at the beginning of their cohabitation and where they are at the end, and then to ask whether either the defender has derived a net economic advantage from the contributions of the applicant or the applicant has suffered a net economic disadvantage in the interests of the defender or any relevant child."

The guiding principles to be taken from this decision and applied by practitioners are as follows:

1. Section 28 is designed to achieve _fairness_. This is not explicitly stated in the legislation, but that was the underlying legislative intention.

2. A _broad_ approach should be adopted, the idea being that imbalances should be corrected and compensation awarded on a "rough and ready valuation". There does not need to be a precise causal connection between contributions made and advantages gained.

3. A capital sum may be awarded even if disadvantage has been suffered to some extent in the pursuer's interests (e.g. the fact that there was some benefit to Miss Gow in selling her property did not preclude her from seeking an award).

Whigham v Owen

The principles established by *Gow v Grant* were followed in the case of *Whigham v Owen*[18] which was heard before Lord Drummond Young in the Court of Session. In this case the parties cohabited for 27 years and had three children together. They had a traditional relationship model. When the parties met, the pursuer was working as a commis chef in a hotel. She gave up work when she became pregnant with the parties' first child. The defender had been working as a plumber when the parties began to cohabit. During the period of the cohabitation, the defender carried out various lucrative property developments in partnership with his brother. He also built up his plumbing business. The pursuer brought up the parties' children, ran the household and assisted in the pursuer's business.

On separation, the pursuer sought a capital sum payment equivalent to fifty percent of the parties' net assets. This was defended on the basis that she had failed to sufficiently quantify her claim.

Lord Drummond Young observed that:

> "*what seems to be envisaged, therefore, is a rough and ready calculation. In deciding what are economic advantages and disadvantages and contributions, the calculation should take into account the factors that are relevant for that purpose in divorce cases. That is not to say that the awards in divorce cases are to be*

---

18 2013 SLT 484

followed, because clearly marriage is a relationship involving a very much more significant commitment than cohabitation. Nevertheless, it appears that the divorce cases may provide some sort of guide as to what are the factors to be taken into account under s.28(3). The approach seems to be based on the proposition that it is difficult to establish precise causal relationships between contributions on one hand and economic advantage or disadvantage on the other; consequently a broad discretion must be exercised in order to achieve overall "fairness". It is clear that most judges and sheriffs feel uncomfortable with the notion of a very broad discretion. I am bound to say that I share that unease. I also have difficulty with the notion of "fairness" in the absence of a proper economic context, but this is perhaps merely an aspect of the breadth of the discretion that the court must exercise."[19]

The pursuer was awarded a sum of £250,000, equivalent to approximately one third of the parties' assets at the date of separation. In making this award, Lord Drummond Young expressed the view that cohabitants should not generally expect to receive a sum equivalent to that which a spouse may be entitled to on divorce. He accepted the defender's submission that awarding a sum equivalent to fifty percent of the net assets was not appropriate. However, he indicated that this case ought to be on the higher end of the scale of possible awards, taking into account the fact that her contributions had enabled the parties to enjoy a generous lifestyle. It was not necessary for precise causal links to be made between the pursuer's contributions and the advantage gained by the defender.

---

19 Para 10

M v S

The case of *M v S*[20] should also be considered. As with *Whigham v Owen*, this case concerned a long cohabitation (nineteen years) and the parties had children together. The case was held at the Court of Session before Lord Ericht. The pursuer based her claim on contributions she had made to the mortgage secured over a farm owned by the defender, which had risen significantly in value during the period of the cohabitation; and on the fact that she had lost earnings by working part time during the cohabitation to bring up the parties' children. At the end of the cohabitation, both parties had seen a marked increase in their net financial positions. The pursuer's net position had gone from £127,500 to £1,085,721; whilst the defender's net position had gone from £102,000 to £5,691,624. The extent of the pursuer's own wealth did not preclude the court from making a substantial award in the pursuer's favour:

> *"The task of the court in deciding whether to exercise its discretion to make an award under section 28 requires consideration of the particular circumstances of the parties in the particular case. Each case turns on its facts. In some cases, one party may have undertaken a domestic role while the other was economically active. In other cases, both will have been economically active. It is important to note that the purpose of section 28 is to redress any economic disadvantage. Its purpose is not the relief of one of the parties from poverty. Accordingly section 28 can apply in situations like the present where both the pursuer and the defender have successful careers and substantial assets."*

This case highlights that the intention of the Act, as interpreted in *Gow v Grant*, is to compensate for unfairness which has arisen as a result of the cohabitation.

---

20 2018 Fam LR 26

Is It Possible to Look At Events Prior To Cohabitation In Determining Section 28 (a) Claims?

This question was considered in the Paisley Sheriff Court case of *W v M*[21]. In that case, part of the capital sum payment which was awarded to the pursuer by the Sheriff at first instance was in recognition of a payment of £1,500 which she had made to the defender <u>prior</u> to the commencement of the parties' cohabitation. The defender appealed unsuccessfully against that decision. The Sheriff Principal noted that there may be some room for ambiguity over the decision. No specific reference had been made to it in *Gow v Grant*. However, ultimately the Sheriff Principal determined that this was a matter best left to the discretion of the Sheriff:

> "*Having regard to the ratio of the Supreme Court in Gow v Grant where a fair outcome was seen as been a key policy aim of the 2006 Act I conclude that the terms of the 2006 Act do not exclude payments made prior to cohabitation commencing being taken into account. With the overall policy aim of the 2006 Act and the ratio of Gow v Grant being to achieve fairness it is appropriate that discretion should rest with the court in determining economic advantage and disadvantage and the relevance of payments or transactions towards that economic advantage and disadvantage. Accordingly I am satisfied as a matter of law in terms of the 2006 Act the sheriff was entitled to have regard to the £1,500 paid over before cohabitation commenced. That accords with the view expressed by Sheriff Miller in Lindsay v Murphy I also find the sheriff was entitled in the exercise of her discretion and in seeking to achieve fairness between the parties to take account of the £1,500 paid prior to the cohabitation commencing in making her award to the pursuer. The sheriff has made an assessment in the round and reached a conclusion aimed at*

21 *W v M* 2016 Fam. L.R. 15

achieving a just outcome. I do not consider she is so plainly wrong that I should interfere with the exercise of her discretion on the matter, particularly where it is looked upon as part of her overall assessment of economic advantage and disadvantage in terms of s.28 of the 2006 Act. There may be other cases where in weighing the matter up the sheriff will reach a conclusion that actions prior to commencement of cohabitation should not be taken into account. It will be a matter to be determined on the facts of a particular case. In the context of the 2006 Act as a whole such a decision is appropriately best left to the discretion of the sheriff."

The point to take from this is that in advising clients, solicitors should not automatically <u>rule out</u> the possibility of seeking awards with reference to money paid out prior to the cohabitation, although, as ever, much will turn on the facts of the particular case.

Contribution to Living Expenses as An Economic Advantage

Can a contribution by one party to the living expenses of the other constitute an "economic advantage" in terms of section 28? This matter was considered by the Sheriff Principal in *Saunders v Martin*[22]. The Sheriff Principal considered that the Sheriff at first instance had not erred in taking into account contributions towards living expenses. Although the views expressed in *Gow v Grant* anticipated a broad-brush approach being taken, the wording of section 28(9) indicates that "economic advantage" <u>includes</u> gains in capital, income and earning capacity, but is not restricted to such gains. It was clear to the Sheriff at first instance that a clear advantage could be derived from contributions to living costs and the legislation should not be afforded an overly narrow interpretation.

---

22 *Saunders v Martin* 2014 Fam. L.R. 86

Lindsay v Murphy

How have the courts dealt with claims in respect of the economic burden of caring for a relevant child? In the main, such claims have been dealt with by taking a broad-brush approach to the likely future costs of providing for children in respect of childcare and other ancillary costs, such as uniform.

In *Lindsay v Murphy*[23] part of the pursuer's claim was for an award under section 28 (2) (b) in respect of caring for the parties' three children. The lion's share of the care fell to her. The Sheriff in that case made a rough and ready allowance for future childcare costs, commenting at paragraph 92 that ' *Any method of quantifying some-thing as broadly expressed as the economic burden of childcare must inevitably be fairly rough and ready. I consider it appropriate to allow for paid childcare costs up to each child's 12th birthday, and to discount these by 25 per cent to allow for holidays, family input and time with friends."*

Smith-Milne v Langler

Should the parties' respective positions at the beginning and end of a cohabitation be compared as a starting point in ascertaining the fairness or otherwise arising from the cohabitation? This question was considered in the Aberdeen Sheriff Court case of *Smith-Milne v Langler*[24]. It was held in that case that "*evidence of the defender's fin-ancial position at the date of cessation of the relationship would be an essential starting point to enable the court to decide what, if any, capital sum should be awarded*"[25].

---

23 *Lindsay v Murphy* 2010 Fam. L.R. 156
24 *Smith-Milne v Langler* Fam LR 58
25 Para 15

It seems therefore to be envisaged that a comparison should be carried out between the parties' positions going into the cohabitation and at the end of cohabitation, to establish whether there is any clear unfairness which may require to be corrected.

On the issue of resources, see also *G v F*[26], in which the Sheriff declined to make any award under section 28 where it was apparent that the defender lacked the resources to meet it.

Interaction With Marriage/Civil Partnership

As well as the fact that the range of awards available to cohabitants are limited, a cohabitant cannot expect to receive an award greater to that which a spouse would receive on divorce. The intention is to redress some imbalance, but not to put them into the same position as that which they would have been in were they in fact married. If there is a concern about becoming financially vulnerable as the result of a relationship, marriage or civil partnership still remains the better protection.

One important point to note is that when we are dealing with divorce in Scotland, there is no mechanism allowing us to take into account the period of cohabitation which preceded the marriage. If one were extremely devious, the right approach, when sensing the imminent breakdown of a cohabiting relationship (with associated hefty financial claim), might be to get hitched. On a subsequent separation the court would then be looking at the period of marriage only and dealing with matters in terms of that legal relationship. A sympathetic court might well be inclined to seek some redress to achieve "fairness" in those circumstances, but would still be restricted

---

26 *G v F* 2011 SLT (Sh Ct) 161

to looking at only the division of "matrimonial property", which may not be extensive.

CHAPTER NINE
SECTION 29 CLAIMS –
TIME LIMITS

A "section 29 claim" is a claim which can be made by the survivor of a cohabiting couple. It fills what was previously an evident gap in the law of succession.

Section 29 claims can <u>only</u> be made where the deceased has died intestate (without a Will). It is important to establish whether there is a Will at an early stage to avoid raising expectations. Having established that the deceased was indeed intestate, swift action must then be taken.

The number one thing for practitioners to remember when dealing with such claims is that the time limit in these circumstances is shorter than that for section 28 claims – perhaps unjustifiably so, given the grief that parties experience in these circumstances. As with section 28 claims, the time limits afforded here rely on the cohabitant being astute enough to seek legal advice at the earliest possible opportunity. The rationale for the shorter time limit is that there requires to be some certainty at an early stage to allow the deceased's estate to be properly administered.

An application to the court must be made with <u>six months</u> of the deceased's death[1], beginning with the date of death. Section 29 claims can be even more hard fought than section 28 claims, with there being competing interests of family members/third parties, perhaps doubt as to the wishes of a deceased and clear evidentiary difficulties. Taking action at an early stage is therefore crucial.

---

1   Section 29(6)

Identifying the Defender

In the event that executors have been appointed, it is appropriate to cite them as the defender(s) to the action.

In the event that there are no executors it may be appropriate to seek decree *cognitionis causa tantum* (an action for declarator of a debt against the deceased's estate). This was considered by Sheriff Holligan at Edinburgh Sheriff Court in *X v A (No.2)*[2]. In that action, the pursuer sought decree *cognitionis causa tantum* and a crave in respect of section 29 of the 2006 Act. The pursuer subsequently removed reference to decree *cognotionis causa tantum* and substituted that for craves against the deceased parents and siblings as executors dative. The defenders opposed the amendment, arguing that it sought to cure a radical incompetency. Essentially their position was that decree *conitionis causa tantum* was not competent for section 29 claims. Such decrees are used to declare a debt due by the estate. By seeking to amend <u>after</u> the six-month time limit for raising a section 29 claim had expired, the pursuer was seeking to cure a defect in their case. Counsel for the pursuer contended that such a decree has two parts: 1) declaring that a debt is due; and 2) making an order for payment. Sheriff Holligan allowed the amendment outwith the six-month time limit, stating that ' *I see no reason to exclude statutory claims from actions of constitution. A claim pursuant to s.29 is a cause of action: it gives a right to pursue a claim. It is not yet a debt against the estate and does not become so until the court has made an award. An action of constitution is flexible enough to comprehend s.29 claims.*"

---

2   *X v A (No. 2)* 2016 SLT (Sh Ct) 411

CHAPTER TEN
SECTION 29 CLAIMS –
ESSENTIAL REQUIREMENTS

This chapter explores the circumstances in which a section 29 claim can be made.

Domicile

A section 29 claim can only be made if the deceased party dies intestate AND immediately prior to the death the deceased was domiciled in Scotland AND was cohabiting with the survivor. For a cohabitant who feels aggrieved that better provision was not made for them in the deceased's Will, that is tough – no claim can be made in terms of this section.

Domicile goes beyond the concept of a party's residence. To be domiciled within a particular jurisdiction, a person must have a settled intention to remain there. Establishing the deceased's domicile may be an extremely difficult task. If challenged, inferences would require to be drawn from their actions and the roots that they had set down prior to their death.

Cohabiting at Death

If the parties had in fact separated prior to the death of one of them and were no longer cohabiting, no section 29 claim could competently be made. Evidence may need to be led at proof in these circumstances where a claim may be vigorously defended by aggrieved family members of the deceased.

CHAPTER ELEVEN
SECTION 29 CLAIMS – WHAT ORDERS CAN BE MADE?

The range of orders available under section 29 differ from those available in terms of section 28.

The court has the authority, by virtue of section 29 (2), to make any or all of the following orders:

- An order for payment of a capital sum from the deceased's net intestate estate;

- An order for transfer of property (including either heritable or moveable property) from the net estate; and

- Such interim order as it thinks fit.

The range of orders is therefore greater than those offered to parties who are separating. The court also has the authority to order that any lump sum payment can be made by way of instalments[1]. It may also vary the date or method of payment on the application of "any party having an interest"[2].

In terms of section 29 (4), it is expressly stated that "*any order or interim order under subsection (2) shall not have the effect of awarding to the survivor an amount which would exceed the amount to which the survivor would have been entitled had the survivor been the spouse or civil partner of the deceased*." Whilst it is documented in case law that the court would not put a cohabitant in the position of a spouse/civil

---

1   Section 29 (7) (b)
2   Section 29 (9)

partner on separation, it is notable that the legislation has made this express provision for claims on death. An appropriate starting point for solicitors would therefore be to calculate the maximum entitlement that a spouse may have, so as to ensure that any award sought by a cohabitant does not breach this threshold.

Factors to Be Taken Into Account

The court is directed to have regard to the following matters by virtue of subsection 3:

a) The size and nature of the deceased's net intestate estate;

b) Any benefit received/due to be received by the survivor on, or in consequence of, the deceased's death; and from somewhere other than the deceased's net intestate estate;

c) The nature and extent of any other rights against/claims on the estate; and

d) "Any other matter the court considers appropriate".

The court is therefore afforded a very wide discretion, as is the case with section 28 claims. The rationale behind this is understandable. Cohabitants, as we have already explored, have not formalised their relationships. In those circumstances, would it be reasonable to impose a formula by which claims on death could be calculated?

The provision at 29(3)(b) is important. Whilst provision may not have been made by way of a Will, cohabitants may be handsomely provided for as nominated beneficiaries of the deceased's pension scheme, or death in service benefits. Such nominations can be extremely valuable and may negate the need for any further financial provision.

Savage v Purches[3]

Savage v Purches concerned an award sought following the death of Mr Savage's cohabitee. The cohabitation had lasted for two and a half years. The whole estate had gone to the deceased's half sister, the deceased having died intestate. The deceased had made provision in a Will (subsequently revoked) for a previous partner, but had failed to make any such provision for Mr Savage. This fact was treated with some significance by the Sheriff as an inference could be led that the deceased had expressly chosen not to make provision for Mr Savage. Mr Savage had already received £120,000 from interests the deceased had in a pension scheme (this was allocated to him on a discretionary basis). The Sheriff determined that no further payment was accordingly due.

In all initial meetings for family law cases the following questions ought to be addressed:

1. Does the client have a Will and Power of Attorney?

2. Have they updated the nominated beneficiary for their pension schemes?

3. Have they nominated a survivor for death in service benefits?

These matters are easy for clients to forget or to put to one side, yet they can have extremely hefty consequences.

---

3 *Savage v Purches* 2009 SLT (Sh Ct) 36

"Net Intestate Estate"

The deceased's net intestate estate is what remains following provision for the following liabilities:

- Inheritance tax;

- Any other liabilities; and

- Legal rights and prior rights (in terms of the Succession (Scotland) Act 1964) of any surviving spouse or any surviving civil partner.[4]

It was observed in *Kerr v Mangan*[5] that it is incorrect to cap section 29 awards at the amount of prior rights which may be available to a spouse/civil partner. The figure could exceed this cap, looking at the amount as a whole to which a spouse might be awarded.

Kerr v Mangan

Property located overseas has been held <u>not</u> to form part of the deceased's net intestate estate for the purposes of section 29. This was examined in some detail in the case of *Kerr v Mangan*[6]. In this case, the pursuer made a claim for a capital sum payment. At the time of death, her cohabitee's estate included sums held in two bank accounts (one in Scotland and the other in the Republic of Ireland) and four plots of land and a bungalow in ROI. There were also various debts due by the estate. The Sheriff at first instance found that the land and property in Ireland could not form part of the "net in-

---

4   Section 29 (10)

5   *Kerr v Mangan* 2014 SLT 866

6   *Kerr v Mangan* 2014 SLT 866

testate estate" for the purposes of section 29 and made an award of just over £5,000. The pursuer appealed to the Sheriff Principal, who found that none of the Irish property could form part of the estate for section 29 purposes, refusing the appeal and reducing the award to nil. The matter then came before the Inner House of the Court of Session. The Inner House concluded that the provisions of section 29 must form part of the law of succession, as opposed to being a "family law" provision. They held that Scottish private law must therefore apply and accordingly found that property held abroad could not be transferred as part of any section 29 award: "*There is no restriction as to what type of property can be transferred but it must be property which the executor dative has power to transfer to the applicant*".[7]

Windram, Applicant

The case of *Windram, Applicant*[8] was heard before Sheriff Scott QC at Jedburgh Sheriff Court in 2009. The applicant had cohabited with the deceased, with whom she had two children. During the cohabitation finances had been merged, but almost all of the assets were held in the sole name of the deceased. Were it not for the possibility to make a claim under section 29, the applicant would have been left with nothing. At the date of the deceased's death, the deceased was domiciled in Scotland, he did not have a Will and the applicant was cohabiting with him. Accordingly, this met the requirements for the court to consider making an award under section 29 of the 2006 Act. Without that, the estate would have been divided equally between the two children. The applicant sought transfer of the family home to her and a capital sum from the estate. This was defended by a curator *ad litem* who had been appointed by the court

---

7   Para 10
8   *Windram, Applicant* 2009 Fam. L.R. 157

to represent the interests of the children. The Sheriff held that the property, furniture and plenishings ought to be transferred to the applicant and that she should receive a capital sum payment of £34,000 from the estate. Specific reference was made in the judgment to the fact that the applicant would be receiving £11,000 less than she would have received had the parties been married. The award which was granted allowed the mortgage over the family home to be repaid by the applicant, but still left the children to inherit the sum of £70,000 each, thus striking a balance between the interests of the applicant and the interests of the children.

Fulwood v O'Halloran

For guidance as the level of specificity required in pleadings see *Fulwood v O'Halloran*[9], in which the parties went to debate due to criticism made by the defender as to the specification and relevancy of the pursuer's pleadings. It was noted by the Sheriff in that case that there needs to be an appropriate degree of specificity to allow the court to carry out a calculation of what a reasonable award might be. This was lacking in the pursuer's pleadings. It is insufficient, for example, to aver that "proceeds of sale of a property" were applied to meet parties' debt during a cohabitation. That does not provide the court with adequate evidence on which to evaluate any award. It was accepted, however, in *Fulwood* that payments made by the applicant to the estate following the deceased's death may fall within the remit of section 29 (3) (d), being "any other matter the court considers appropriate" in considering whether to make an order under section 29.

---

9 *Fulwood v O'Halloran* 2014 WL 1097050

CHAPTER TWELVE
OTHER MATTERS TO CONSIDER

Tax

From a risk management perspective, it is crucial to have a working knowledge of the tax issues which may crop up when assisting parties in disentangling a relationship. If nothing else the fact that there *may* be tax implications in any settlement should at least be flagged to ensure that appropriate advice is sought.

Capital Gains Tax is one to flag in almost all family law cases that may cross your desk. Liability for Capital Gains Tax (CGT) may arise on the disposal of any asset which has increased in value between the date of acquisition and the date of disposal (subject to certain exceptions). Houses and shareholdings are the categories of assets most likely to cause difficulty for cohabitants under these headings. For parties who are married or in a civil partnership, no CGT will be payable on assets transferred between the spouses/civil partners during the marriage/civil partnership. This applies even after separation, provided that these transfers take place within the tax year of separation. This exception is not, however, extended to cohabitants.

To give an example under this heading:

- A and B have a home in Aberdeen which they own in joint names. They live there and cohabit together for three years. They also purchase, during that period, a holiday home on Skye. The holiday home on Skye is also in joint names. After three years of blissful cohabiting life, B dumps A. Since acquisition, the home in Aberdeen has increased in value by £50,000. The property on Skye has increased by £50,000 as well.

- After some negotiation, A and B agree that the house in which they live together will be transferred into B's sole name. The Skye property will be transferred to A. B feels that he is getting a great deal, but what is the CGT position?

- There will be <u>no</u> Capital Gains Tax payable by A. This is because she is "disposing of" her main residence. There is a specific exemption for such disposals.

- B starts to feel considerably less smug when he realises that there <u>will</u> be CGT payable by him on the transfer of his half share of the Skye property to A. This is because the Skye property is not and has never been his main residence and accordingly that exemption does not apply. There are no specific exemptions in place for cohabiting parties. B will need to head straight to a tax adviser to work out what annual allowances he may be able to use to mitigate the cost.

Inheritance Tax (IHT) may also rear its head when considering what may be payable following a cohabiting person's death. There are numerous exemptions and allowances in place for spouses and civil partners. These do not apply to cohabitants.

Cohabitants also need to be aware of falling foul of the "Additional Dwelling Supplement" (ADS). ADS is tax charged on the acquisition of any property beyond a person's main residence, where the property is purchased for £40,000 or more. The tax charged on such an acquisition is 4% of the purchase price. It can be easy for cohabitants to find themselves unexpectedly liable for this charge. Take the following scenario:

- A and B each own their own property. House A is A's "main residence". House B is B's "main residence".

- A sells House A. A purchases House C in his sole name. A thinks this is fine, as no ADS is payable where A is simply re-placing his main residence (house A) with a new one (house C).

- However, A and B both move into house C. B also retains house B. ADS is chargeable even though B's name does not appear on the title deed to house C.

If in doubt, advise your clients to obtain tax advice before making any changes to the way in which their assets are held. Tax advice and family law advice ought to be dovetailed: what makes good tax advice often does not make good family law advice, and vice versa.

Property Law

It is wise to consider whether dealing with matters by applying the 2006 Act principles is always necessary, or whether it may be preferable to deal with matters in some other way.

Some couples setting up home together for the first time may choose to avoid the expense of a pre cohabitation agreement and instead take title to a property purchased by them in unequal shares, reflective of their intended contributions. This arguably leaves one or both of those parties exposed, but it is an option which we see having been exercised on occasion. Linked to that, it is important to check exactly how title has been taken if there is any doubt in the mind of your client. Where title has been taken in unequal shares, this would not negate an argument down the line based on any perceived economic advantage or disadvantage, although it would certainly make for a more difficult starting point.

If you are dealing with a client whose former partner is adopting the "ostrich approach", sitting pretty in a jointly owned property and your client wants their share of the equity out, a straightforward answer might be to raise an action for division and sale. This would particularly be recommended if your client has no good argument to receive a greater than 50% share of the property (assuming title is held equally) and a section 28 claim is time barred. If a section 28 claim is not yet time barred and there is a prospect of the other party making such a claim, there is a possibility of the defender being able to persuade the court to sist the division and sale action until such time as the section 28 claim has been determined.

CHAPTER THIRTEEN
UNJUSTIFIED ENRICHMENT

It is accepted in Scots Law that an "enrichment" is likely to be unjustified where there is no legal basis for the enrichment. An example of this might be where person A pays towards the purchase price of a property owned solely by B in the belief that parties will live in the property together, but that is not what actually goes on to occur. If unjustified enrichment is established, this can be corrected by an action for repetition (repayment), restitution (property being returned) or recompense (otherwise correcting the enrichment which has been unjustly created).

The test for establishing unjustified enrichment is usefully spelled out in the narration of the pursuer's submission at paragraph 11 of the Inner House's judgment in *Pert v McCaffrey* as follows:

> "*The test was now in four parts: (1) the defender had to be enriched; (2) the enrichment had to be at the pursuer's expense; (3) there had to be an absence of legal justification for the enrichment; and (4) it had to be equitable for the court to compel the redress of that enrichment (equity being more of a defence).*"[1]

When Can an Unjustified Enrichment Claim Be Used?

It was held in *Courtney's Exxs v Campbell*[2] that a claim for unjustified enrichment could not be brought in circumstances where there would have been an alternative remedy available to the pursuer in terms of section 28 of the 2006 Act, the one-year time limit for

---

1   *Pert v McCaffrey*, 2020 SLT 225, para 11
2   *Courtney's Exxs v Campbell* 2017 SCLR 187

which had elapsed. Unjustified enrichment claims are time barred only after a five-year period has elapsed[3]. The action was brought by the executors of Mr Courtney, who had cohabited with the Defender from 2010 to 2013. A house had been purchased in the sole name of the Defender. The deceased had made payments to the Defender totalling £100,000. The executors indicated that the payments were made in the belief by the deceased that the property was in joint names and that he would benefit from those payments by living in the property together with the Defender. As it happened, the cohabiting parties separated prior to the deceased's death. The deceased was not aware that he could make a 2006 Act claim and accordingly none was brought. The executors therefore claimed for unjustified enrichment. This was defended on the principle of "subsidiarity", which essentially means that a claim cannot be made where there was an alternative remedy available which was not exercised. Lord Beckett held that *"on the basis that the deceased had a remedy under the 2006 Act which he failed to pursue, and not being satisfied that there are special and strong circumstances, I conclude that the pursuers have not pled a case which entitles them to the remedy they seek".*[4]

This decision was superseded by the Inner House judgment in *Pert v McCaffrey*[5], holding at paragraph 24 that:

> *"The power of the court [in section 28 claims] is one of weighing up the various economic advantages and disadvantages and making a judgment, essentially of a discretionary nature, on whether a capital sum ought to be awarded. In making that assessment, it must be assumed that the ordinary legal remedies open to the parties, such as to secure particular property which is owned by them, have been, or can be, exercised. Put another way, the court*

---

3 Prescription & Limitation (Scotland) Act 1973, Sched. 1, Para 1(b)

4 Para 7

5 *Pert v McCaffrey* 2020 SLT 225

must presuppose that the pursuer cannot obtain payment from the defender other than by utilising the statutory provisions of the 2006 Act. Seen in that light, s.28 is not a remedy which is alternative to an action for recompense but one which is additional to any common law remedy otherwise available. The failure to exercise the right to make an application under s.28 timeously does not bar the use of such remedies. In this respect the court must disagree with Courtney's Exrs v Campbell (at 2017 S.C.L.R., p.399, para.70)."

Accordingly, it is established that it is possible to make a claim for unjustified enrichment in circumstances where section 28 claims are no longer available due to the passage of time. That being said, such remedies can only be sought where the test for unjustified enrichment is met and any unjustified enrichment claim has not prescribed. It was contended for the Pursuer in *Pert* that the prescription period for unjustified enrichment had only commenced when the Defender indicated that he did not intend to adhere to the agreement they had previously reached that he would make no claim on the parties' jointly owned property no separation; this argument did not find merit with the court, who found that it had begun to prescribe on the date of the parties' separation.

CHAPTER FOURTEEN
ADVISING CLIENTS

Prior To Cohabitation

Unfortunately, relatively few people would consider seeing a solicitor prior to commencing their cohabitation. It is likewise rare for people to seek advice from a family lawyer prior to entering into a marriage or civil partnership which are formalised relationships and have a more evident set of legal consequences, so perhaps we should not be surprised by this.

Those who do come into the office seeking advice prior to cohabitation are often needled into doing so by a concerned parent or grandparent. This may be in circumstances where the individual in question is due to receive a healthy deposit for a house in which they intend to live with their beloved, or where there is an intention to pass down wealth through the family whilst ensuring that wealth is protected.

Where parties are seeking advice prior to cohabitation, the following should be considered:

- Where are they habitually resident and domiciled?

- Where do they intend to cohabit? If neither party is domiciled in Scotland, they intend to leave imminently and have no plans to return, they are unlikely to be able to make claims (in either direction) under the Family Law (Scotland) Act 2006. The ins and outs of this ought to be discussed.

- Are they cohabiting for a short period with a view to marrying imminently (as with engaged couples)? If so, it may not be necessary to go to the expense of putting together a pre cohabitation agreement, or alternatively an agreement may be reached which encompasses both the period of cohabitation and the following marriage.

• What is the asset and income position of each of the parties? A detailed analysis of this should be undertaken to ascertain whether it is recommended for the parties to enter into a pre cohabitation agreement and if so, how detailed that agreement requires to be.

• Where a client is clear that they do not wish to enter into a pre cohabitation agreement, advice will need to be tendered as to keeping good paper trails to evidence any arguments they may need to contend with down the line.

• The time limits for the making of claims ought to be highlighted. This includes tendering advice as to how far in advance of the expiry of the time limit they ought to see their solicitor if they are to allow sufficient time for negotiation prior to the raising and service of an action.

• Those who intend to cohabit, as with all individuals, should be advised to put a Will in place. Having a Will protects their estate from section 29 claims, which can only be made in the event of intestacy.

Cohabitation Agreements

Cohabitation agreements can be entered into prior to, during or after cohabitation and are essentially governed by contract law. There is authority in Scotland for the proposition that such contracts will be treated as binding. Pre cohabitation agreements are the best protection that we can offer to clients at present (other than the option of deciding not to cohabit).

Dispute Resolution Models

Whilst keeping a strict eye on the calendar to ensure that time limits for the making of claims are not missed, it is almost always preferable for privately funded clients to resolve matters outwith court, particularly given the hugely discretionary nature of awards available under the 2006 Act and the inherent risk that brings.

Practitioners should bear in mind that mediation, arbitration and the collaborative models of dispute resolution are all open to cohabitants and can often help clients to work towards efficient and creative solutions. There is provision at section 29A of the 2006 Act for a short extension of the time limits (in certain circumstances) for section 28 and section 29 claims where the parties are engaged in cross-border mediation.

CHAPTER FIFTEEN
THE FUTURE OF SCOTS LAW
ON COHABITATION?

It seems evident that further clarity as to how 2006 Act cases should be decided would be of assistance to practitioners and the public. Increased public awareness of the implications of moving one's beloved into the home would be helpful. An area of law that relies largely on the discretion of an individual decision maker seems a risky business for all concerned: Sheriffs are not envied in those circumstances.

As further households become "cohabiting" ones, there are questions to be answered as to whether the current law provides adequate protection, or whether further updating is required. The original recommendations which led to the 2006 Act legislation were made in 1992, a gap of fourteen years. The Scottish Law Commission's further consultation on Cohabitation took place in 2020, with a report due to be issued in 2021. The consultation report is well worth a read. Comparisons are drawn between Scots Law and the position of cohabitants in other (non-UK) jurisdictions and although not the subject of this book, certainly provide ample ideas as to how cohabitation law in Scotland may evolve. It is to be hoped that if further changes are recommended they may take a little less time to make their way into our law.

Solicitors at present are seeing a plethora of nuisance claims. With the legal position being so reliant on a Sheriff's discretion, it is very difficult to advise a client where a claim is relatively small and there is a risk of there being a very wide range of potential awards. In such circumstances, the right commercial approach is often for the client to write a cheque to buy off the risk.

Should parties have the option to opt in/out of a cohabitation re-gime, or does this undermine the concept of safeguarding the vulner-able? Should there be a wider range of financial remedies available to cohabitants? Is the definition of "cohabitant" itself outdated? What about couples living "apart together"? These questions and more have all been posed by the SLC consultation, so it seems likely that there may be some further movement in Scottish cohabitation law in the future.

MORE BOOKS BY
LAW BRIEF PUBLISHING

A selection of our other titles available now:-

'Covid-19, Homeworking and the Law – The Essential Guide to Employment and GDPR Issues' by Forbes Solicitors
'Covid-19, Force Majeure and Frustration of Contracts – The Essential Guide' by Keith Markham
'Covid-19 and Criminal Law – The Essential Guide' by Ramya Nagesh
'Covid-19 and Family Law in England and Wales – The Essential Guide' by Safda Mahmood
'Covid-19 and the Implications for Planning Law – The Essential Guide' by Bob Mc Geady & Meyric Lewis
'Covid-19, Residential Property, Equity Release and Enfranchisement – The Essential Guide' by Paul Sams and Louise Uphill
'Covid-19, Brexit and the Law of Commercial Leases – The Essential Guide' by Mark Shelton
'Covid-19 and the Law Relating to Food in the UK and Republic of Ireland – The Essential Guide' by Ian Thomas
'A Practical Guide to the General Data Protection Regulation (GDPR) – 2nd Edition' by Keith Markham
'Ellis on Credit Hire – Sixth Edition' by Aidan Ellis & Tim Kevan
'A Practical Guide to Working with Litigants in Person and McKenzie Friends in Family Cases' by Stuart Barlow
'Protecting Unregistered Brands: A Practical Guide to the Law of Passing Off' by Lorna Brazell
'A Practical Guide to Secondary Liability and Joint Enterprise Post-Jogee' by Joanne Cecil & James Mehigan

'A Practical Guide to Chronic Pain Claims' by Pankaj Madan
'A Practical Guide to Claims Arising from Fatal Accidents' by James Patience
'A Practical Guide to Subtle Brain Injury Claims' by Pankaj Madan

These books and more are available to order online direct from the publisher at www.lawbriefpublishing.com, where you can also read free sample chapters. For any queries, contact us on 0844 587 2383 or mail@lawbriefpublishing.com.

Our books are also usually in stock at www.amazon.co.uk with free next day delivery for Prime members, and at good legal bookshops such as Wildy & Sons.

We are regularly launching new books in our series of practical day-to-day practitioners' guides. Visit our website and join our free newsletter to be kept informed and to receive special offers, free chapters, etc.

You can also follow us on Twitter at www.twitter.com/lawbriefpub.

Printed in Great Britain
by Amazon